T0166406

SLEEP DEPRIVATION CHAMBER

SLEEP DEPRIVATION CHAMBER

A THEATRE PIECE

ADAM P. KENNEDY AND
ADRIENNE KENNEDY

THEATRE COMMUNICATIONS GROUP

Sleep Deprivation Chamber is published by Theatre Communications Group, Inc., 355 Lexington Ave., New York, NY 10017-0217.

Kennedy, Adam (Adam P.)
Sleep deprivation chamber / by Adam and Adrienne Kennedy.
ISBN 1–55936–126–3
1. Afro-American men—Virginia—Drama. 2. Mothers and sons—Virginia—Drama. 3. Police brutality—Virginia—Drama.
4. Suburban life—Virginia—Drama.
I. Kennedy, Adrienne. II. Title.
PS3561. E42518S58   1996
812'.54—dc20   96–35079
    CIP

Cover art by Susan Johann
Cover design by Susan Mitchell
Book design by Lisa Govan

First Edition, November 1996
Second Printing, March 2014

To all the people who believed in me and supported the Kennedy family—thank you. All the incredible letters on my behalf made me realize how truly blessed I am. They provided me with a great deal of strength and power during a very difficult time.

Sometimes in the midst of great tragedy one realizes the enormous amount of love and faith that surrounds them. My mom and dad, the greatest parents in the world, guided me with their strength, support, courage, determination and great dignity—I couldn't have made it without them. To Roger Adelman and Tom Foltz, two great lawyers who outsmarted the police and the district attorney's office at every turn. To Duane Grier—my brother in spirit who endured with me, to my brother Joe, Aunt Mary, Harriet Jones, Claire Hunkin, Sam Peabody, Marty and Gus Trowbridge, Stephen Trowbridge, Jean Stein and my grandmothers, Etta Hawkins and Jessie Hunkin.

A very special thanks to Michael Kahn for his brilliant vision and the whole cast, especially Kevin Carroll. To Renee and my daughter Dori—hopefully by the time she reaches adulthood our society will have come to grips with, and defeated, the evils of racism in America.

And finally, I would like to dedicate this book to all the black American men who shared with me their own horrible experiences with the police—it is a sobering reality that my experience is such a common one.

—*Adam P. Kennedy*

For friends who wrote the letters . . . and those who did more . . . Mary K. Carter, Sam Peabody, Jean Stein, Marty and Gus Trowbridge, Charles Robb's office staff and my son, Joe, who gave me advice on serenity. . . . And for Michael Kahn and his breathtaking directing.

—*Adrienne Kennedy*

SLEEP DEPRIVATION CHAMBER

The world premiere of *Sleep Deprivation Chamber* was presented February–March 1996 by Signature Theatre Company in New York City and was performed on the stage of the Public Theater/New York Shakespeare Festival. The production was directed by Michael Kahn, with sets by E. David Cosier, lights by Jeffrey S. Koger, sound by Jim van Bergen and costumes by Teresa Snider-Stein and Jonathan Green. The cast was as follows:

SUZANNE	Trazana Beverley
TEDDY	Kevin T. Carroll
MARCH	Grafton Trew
DAVID ALEXANDER	Willie C. Carpenter
MR. EDELSTEIN	Paul Geier
MS. WAGNER	Glynis Bell
OFFICER HOLZER	Jonathan Fried
ENSEMBLE	Mark Gorman, Ben Hersey, Leslie Silva, Bo Smith, Jacques Henri Taylor

Antioch College, Yellow Springs, Ohio
Ohio Theatre, Cleveland, Ohio
Hotel, Washington, D.C.
Courtroom in Virginia

TIME

Two years ago

CHARACTERS

(Cast of ten to twelve actors)

SUZANNE ALEXANDER, Teddy's mother, a writer
TEDDY, a senior at Antioch College
MARCH ALEXANDER, Teddy's uncle
DAVID ALEXANDER, Teddy's father, head of Africa/USA

The police, lawyers, Patrice, David Jr., the cousin, the student
cast of a play, etc., are all played interchangeably by the same
actors.

Winter. Antioch College Theatre Department. Backstage with a view of the rehearsal hall and stage. In the rehearsal hall is a long table. The Student Cast sits with scripts and books, their voices are muted. The rehearsal hall and backstage are almost dark.

Suzanne sits at a dressing table writing.

STUDENT CAST: Ophelia, betrayal, disillusionment.

(Suzanne looks toward doorway at the end of the rehearsal hall, she's an African-American writer, mid-fifties. She wears winter coat, scarf.)

STUDENT CAST: Ophelia, betrayal, disillusionment.

(Through the door at the end of the rehearsal hall comes Teddy, Suzanne's son. He is a slight young man, twenty-one, sallow skin like his mother's, black hair already thinning, glasses, wearing rehearsal clothes. He joins Student Cast at table. He is the director.)

STUDENT CAST: The murder of the sleeping king.

(Suzanne puts her head down on the dressing table.)

STUDENT CAST: Asleep at the moment of his murder.

(Suzanne falls asleep. Her voice narrates dream sequence. All dream sequences have fragments of the dream acted out onstage. These fragments are identified here by DREAM SCENE.*)*

SUZANNE: Teddy was accused of murdering a French king again. And while he was in jail in Virginia (after being condemned) Teddy's right hand was cut off. And his body was drawn in sunder and dismembered by five horses and his carcass and quarters cast into a fire and consumed to ashes and the ashes scattered to the wind while I yelled at the killers.

DREAM SCENE: *(Teddy's body is drawn in sunder and dismembered, his carcass cast into a fire.)*

SUZANNE: I've been to Concord and read Thoreau and Emerson and my grandmother went to church twice a week and our family has worked hard for justice.
    Please believe me, I held up a photograph of my father's church. *(Holds up a photograph of her father's church)*

(She walks, writes.)

SUZANNE:
    Dear County Manager:
        Again I write—
        That morning in January Patrice called me crying, explaining how they had been sleeping when the sound

of police sirens awakened them. The room appeared aflame with light and then a scream. It was Teddy. In the middle of that same night I dreamed about men living underneath the Westside Highway at 96th Street.

(Pause)

My children, Patrice and Teddy, were visiting their father in Arlington.

(Light goes to Teddy sitting at the rehearsal table)

What did I do, he screamed.

STUDENT ACTOR:

"I am thy father's spirit
Doomed for a certain time to walk the night
And for the day confined to fast in fires
Till the foul crimes done in my days of nature
Are burnt and purged away. . . ."

(Light on Teddy. He remembers as Suzanne writes.)

SUZANNE:

Dear Governor Wilder:

My name is Suzanne Alexander. I am a black writer. I have written you once before in February. I am writing to you again about the Arlington, Virginia Police Department.

(Scene of Teddy and Police Officer. Flashing red and white lights and the image of a car. A white Officer moves toward Teddy.)

TEDDY: Officer, what seems to be the problem? Can I help you?
OFFICER: Get back in the car.
TEDDY: Officer, what seems to be the problem? I live here, this is my house. Can I help you? *(Fade)*

(Light on Suzanne.)

SUZANNE *(Continues letter to Governor Wilder)*:
We are an outstanding black American family. My former husband, David, is head of Africa/USA. My plays and stories are published and taught widely.

We are now a grieved family. Our son is being persecuted by the Arlington Police Department just as surely as happened in the Deep South in the 1930s or during Emmett Till's time.

On Friday night, January 11, my son, a fine citizen who has never been in any trouble whatsoever, was knocked to the ground and beaten in the face, kicked repeatedly in the chest and stomach and dragged in the mud by an Arlington Virginia policeman whose name is Holzer. This occurred in his father's front yard on Riverdale Street in Arlington. My son was stopped because he had a taillight out on his car. There was no further provocation from him. The Arlington police arrested my son, then concocted a totally false story and charges, and charged him with assault and battery.

This is the height of persecution of a black male with tactics of the Deep South of the time 1930s and overtones of Emmett Till. My son has never been in any trouble at all. He is a fine citizen and student at Antioch College. Please look into the Arlington Police Department and its racial persecution of our son and our family. We are grieved and shocked. We want these false charges dismissed.

> *Suzanne Alexander*
> *Dr. David Alexander*
> *Patrice Alexander*
> *David Alexander, Jr.*

P.S.

Ever since he'd been a child he has been described by everyone as brilliant. He's always wanted to be a theatre director-slash-writer and actor. But like David, he has a scholarly side and his essays on culture, race, theatre and literature are already published by a college journal in New York. This is his senior year at Antioch.

(Teddy thinking. Sees himself standing in a dark driveway in handcuffs, his face swollen, being questioned by "Unseen Questioner." Student Cast remains on stage silently rehearsing.)

UNSEEN QUESTIONER: So when he hit you, you didn't go to the ground?

TEDDY: I went to the ground when he first hit me and then that's when he proceeded to drag me across the driveway while he was kicking me and hitting me.

UNSEEN QUESTIONER: Well, what position were you in when he first started to drag you?

TEDDY: I was basically crouched down on the ground.

UNSEEN QUESTIONER: You were in a crouch?

TEDDY: Well, crouch might—I was bending when he hit me I sort of—I moved to the ground—I was bending at the knees and he put his hand behind me and proceeded to drag me across, all right.

UNSEEN QUESTIONER: What part of you was dragging on the ground if—

TEDDY: My legs were dragging on the ground. I mean, you could—from my pants—from the dirt and the scuffle marks on my pants—my—both my jackets were torn. I was being just drug across the driveway.

UNSEEN QUESTIONER: Well, are you lying on—totally extended on your side or are you—is he dragging you in your crouch?

TEDDY: He's dragging—I'm dragging me—I am sort of diagonal. All right. My—I am in sort of a crouch-type position and crunched down because he's trying to force me to the ground and he's kicking me and punching me. But yet, he's also pulling me from the back of the car diagonally across to . . . to the end of the driveway.

UNSEEN QUESTIONER: Did you say anything to him at this time?

TEDDY: It's very difficult to say anything when a guy is kicking you and punching you in your face and your stomach and your back.

UNSEEN QUESTIONER: How about like, stop it or don't hit me or you're hurting me? Did you say anything to him?

TEDDY: No, I didn't say anything at that point to Officer Holzer while he was dragging me and kicking me. Because I was in a state—I was so stunned—so surprised that he was doing this. I mean, I was just—I couldn't believe that . . .

(Fade. The Student Cast breaks from rehearsal and vanishes through the rear door.)

———

(Suzanne walks onto the stage and sits across from Teddy at the table. Behind them is a stage and set of Hamlet *resembling a scene from an Orson Welles piece, shadows, dark spaces, little furnishings.)*

TEDDY: Mom, what else can we do to find Uncle March?

SUZANNE: I've hired a detective and every day my friend, Maynard, editor of the *Oakland Tribune*, writes about March. I don't know what else to do until your criminal suit is over. I'll go to California. Patrice has moved into his cottage from her own apartment.

TEDDY: You do believe Uncle March is alive?

SUZANNE: Yes. He's wandered off before.

Teddy, are you preparing for all your meetings? Back-stage I write again to Robb, Warner, Wilder. I'm sending them photographs of you as a child in Ghana. I dreamed about March last night and you too. We were all at Stanford.

(Teddy thinks. He again is questioned by Unseen Questioner.)

TEDDY: Yes, I pulled over—I pulled into the driveway which was—there were several cars on my left so I could not pull—I just pulled into the driveway which was about fifty feet, sixty feet away and I was, you know, going down the hill—there's a hill—going fifteen miles an hour, it took me several seconds.

UNSEEN QUESTIONER: So you didn't stop your car when the emergency light—

TEDDY: Oh, yes I did.

UNSEEN QUESTIONER: How much time transpired between the time the emergency lights came on and you brought your vehicle to a stop in the driveway?

TEDDY: About ten seconds.

UNSEEN QUESTIONER: How fast were you going?

TEDDY: Fifteen miles an hour.

UNSEEN QUESTIONER: How far were you from your driveway when you saw those emergency lights?

TEDDY: I would say approximately fifty feet or so.

UNSEEN QUESTIONER: Then what happened?

TEDDY: I pulled the car into the driveway. I parked the car. I got out of the vehicle, closed the door. I saw that there was a police officer who had gotten out of his . . .

(Fade.)

=====

SUZANNE *(Narrates Dream Scene)*: My brother-in-law, March, and I are sitting on the small terrace outside the cottage beneath the tree. I stare at the red poison berries. Beyond, men play golf. He writes in the Scarlet Fever List.

DREAM SCENE: *(Suzanne and March sitting on terrace. A white sign on cottage door says: "Do Not Enter." Yellow tapes: "Crime Scene.")*

MARCH: Great storms will be. This day there are great storms of wind, overturned trees, barns and houses, even forests. We live near the epicenter.

SUZANNE *(Staring at the red berry tree)*: We drink cappuccino. It is the day after the 1989 earthquake. Part of the Bay Bridge has fallen. There is another shock, the radio says there will be approximately three hundred aftershocks in the next two months. But if the big one doesn't come before Christmas, then it probably won't. All around us are yellow tapes that say "Crime Scene." A white sign on the door of the cottage says, "Do Not Enter Property: Will be examined for damage, October 30."

(Suzanne stands, enters living room amidst fallen furniture. Teddy is being kicked in the stomach by the Virginia police. His clothes are covered with mud, his face swelling from the blows by the policeman's elbow.)

SUZANNE: I offer the Policeman poison.
TEDDY *(Crying out as they kick him)*: Mom, help me.

(They handcuff Teddy and take him away in a paddy wagon. Silence.)

TEDDY: Dad talked to a lawyer today in Washington.

====

(David Alexander, a handsome man in his mid-sixties, being questioned by an unseen Lawyer for the prosecution.)

DAVID ALEXANDER: Well, the first thing I saw, when I went out, he was standing there, and then I saw an officer with a gun drawn.

LAWYER: You saw an officer with a gun drawn?

DAVID ALEXANDER: Yes, in that stance.

LAWYER: Would you describe the officer?

DAVID ALEXANDER: Well, black female.

LAWYER: Did you ever learn that officer's name?

DAVID ALEXANDER: Yes.

LAWYER: What was her name?

DAVID ALEXANDER: Officer Summers.

LAWYER: Could you describe the weapon?

DAVID ALEXANDER: No.

LAWYER: Have you ever been in the military?

DAVID ALEXANDER: Yes.

LAWYER: What branch of the service?

DAVID ALEXANDER: I was in the Medical Service Corps, in Korea.

LAWYER: Did you have any basic military training, as opposed to the medical training?

DAVID ALEXANDER: Yes, I had basic training.

LAWYER: What branch or service?

DAVID ALEXANDER: Well, I was trained in the infantry.

LAWYER: Army?

DAVID ALEXANDER: No, I was in the Medical Service Corps, stationed for training at Camp Pickett. We went through regular basic training.

LAWYER: Did you ever fire a .45 or have any familiarity with a .45?

DAVID ALEXANDER: No.

LAWYER: Did you ever fire an M1, M14, M16?

DAVID ALEXANDER: M1, yes.

LAWYER: Can you describe, at all, the weapon that you say that the female officer had drawn?

DAVID ALEXANDER: I couldn't describe it.

LAWYER: Do you know what color it was?

DAVID ALEXANDER: No.

LAWYER: Was it black? Silver? Gold?

DAVID ALEXANDER: I have no idea.

LAWYER: Do you know the difference between a revolver and an automatic? The revolver has the cylinder where the bullets go and—

DAVID ALEXANDER: No, no.

LAWYER: Where was the officer, with the drawn gun, when you saw her?

DAVID ALEXANDER: She was standing in the yard.

LAWYER: Who was she pointing the gun at?

DAVID ALEXANDER: Well, I'm not sure.

LAWYER: Who—

DAVID ALEXANDER: My—my son was standing there with the camera. She would have been off to my left. So, when I came out, that's the first thing I saw. I saw him with the camera, and I saw her with a gun.

LAWYER: Did you ever view the video that your other son shot?

DAVID ALEXANDER: Yes.

LAWYER: Was she a black police officer, female-type, with a drawn weapon, in the video?

DAVID ALEXANDER: No—I don't know.

LAWYER: Did you ever ask any other family member if they saw a police officer with a drawn gun?

DAVID ALEXANDER: No, I'm not sure whether my son did or not. I don't know.

LAWYER: My question was, did you ever ask any other members of your family—

═══

(The Student Cast returns to rehearsal.
Suzanne goes back to dressing room. Again, as she writes
there are muted voices of the Student Cast discussing Hamlet.*)*

STUDENT CAST *(In unison)*: The murder of the sleeping king.

SUZANNE:
Dear Senator:
I write you again . . .

(Light on Teddy sitting at rehearsal table. One of the Student
Cast is on stage.)

TEDDY *(Thinking as he watches Student Actor on stage do silent*
monologue): My Uncle March who has done so much to
help fight for racial equality in the United States, his teach-
ing, his books, now at sixty-four he suffers memory lapses
and often seems forgotten by younger activists and educa-
tors. Many times he sits alone on the round stone seat near
the Stanford post office. Sometimes he walks with St. Clair
Drake. Few of the black students know of his role in histo-
ry with Fanon, Nkrumah. Now he disappears and wanders
in the Palo Alto hills.

DREAM SCENE: *(March sits on a round stone seat near the*
Stanford Post Office. He stands and walks joined by St. Clair
Drake, a famous scholar. March disappears wandering
toward the Palo Alto hills. Fade.)

SUZANNE:
Dear Congressman:
My daughter, Patrice, a lecturer at Stanford, says
bugloss will console my heart and memory and engen-

der good blood and void the madness and frenzy I feel.

STUDENT CAST: Asleep at the moment of his murder.

(Teddy, thinking, hears Unseen Questioner.)

TEDDY: I asked him, I said, "Officer what seems to be the problem? Can I help you?"

And then he yelled very loudly, "Get back in your car."

And I said to him, I said, "Officer, what seems to be the problem? I live here, this is my house. Can I help you?"

And he yelled again, "Get back in the car."

UNSEEN QUESTIONER: When the police officer first told you to get back in the car, did you comply?

TEDDY: No.

UNSEEN QUESTIONER: Why not?

TEDDY: Because I was trying to engage him in a civil conversation and I just wanted to find out what seemed to be the problem.

UNSEEN QUESTIONER: When you saw the—

TEDDY: I was in my own driveway at my own house in a calm voice trying to ask him what was wrong. I didn't see that that was a problem.

UNSEEN QUESTIONER: Well, the emergency lights came on when you were out on the road. Is that correct?

TEDDY: Down the hill. Yes.

UNSEEN QUESTIONER: And at that time did you think that the police officer was trying to get you to stop?

TEDDY: Yes. And that's where I stopped.

UNSEEN QUESTIONER: Is there any reason that you didn't stop right there in the road instead of driving into your driveway?

TEDDY: Again, there were—the house next to us there were several cars right there and it was a natural reaction for me to turn in my driveway.

I do it, you know, I've done it hundreds, hundreds of times. So, it seemed to me natural just to pull in, pull into the driveway.

UNSEEN QUESTIONER: Wasn't there space all in front of your house to park where the police cruisers all subsequently parked?

TEDDY: Yes. There was space.

UNSEEN QUESTIONER: Okay.

TEDDY: In front of the house. In front of the house, next to it, no there wasn't. That's when I first saw the lights.

UNSEEN QUESTIONER: Weren't you at all afraid that you might be stopped for some type of criminal offense when the police first put on their emergency lights?

TEDDY: No.

UNSEEN QUESTIONER: Did you take a step toward your house at any point after the—after you parked your car?

TEDDY: No.

UNSEEN QUESTIONER: At any time did you take a step toward your house? Or try and leave the area?

TEDDY: No.

UNSEEN QUESTIONER: What happened after the officer told you the second time to get back in the car?

TEDDY: I said, "Officer what seems to be the problem? Can I help you? This is my house, I live here."

I pulled the car latch and began to open the door. And before I could open the door all the way, Officer Holzer had made his way to the back of the Granada. He said, "Come back here."

UNSEEN QUESTIONER: What did you say?

TEDDY: I closed the door and I made my way to the back of the car.

UNSEEN QUESTIONER: Did you say anything?

TEDDY: No.

UNSEEN QUESTIONER: Then what happened?

TEDDY: I got to the back of the car. I was moving very slowly toward him. He was obviously very—he was hostile. So I was concerned. We got—we were—when I got to the end of the car he was standing there and he grabbed my right hand, forcibly by the wrist, and tried to yank me down. And I pulled my hand away and I said, "Don't touch me."

And at that moment, he then struck me in my face with his hand or with a flashlight and knocked me to the ground.

UNSEEN QUESTIONER: Well, which?

TEDDY: I don't know. It was—it was just a very heavy object. It was either his fist or his flashlight.

UNSEEN QUESTIONER: Couldn't you see?

TEDDY: When I pulled my hand away, I was looking to the right. I mean his hand came out, his right hand came and just hit me and I couldn't see it. He basically, I would use the word sucker punched me.

UNSEEN QUESTIONER: Which hand did he have the flashlight in?

TEDDY: His right hand.

UNSEEN QUESTIONER: Which hand did he hit you with?

TEDDY: His right hand.

UNSEEN QUESTIONER: What happened after you were struck?

TEDDY: I fell to the ground. He then proceeded to grab me and drag me across my driveway at a diagonal angle while he was proceeding to kick me in my stomach and my back and punch me repeatedly.

(Fade.)

━━━

(Teddy remembers: Lawyers, officers, David Alexander, David Jr. and he are seated at a table with a black lawyer.)

TEDDY: Her office was in a small brownstone in the black section of Alexandria and we must have easily waited twenty-five to thirty minutes before we were led downstairs into this gloomy basement office.

She was in her forties. After I told her what happened, she asked very few questions about the evening and acted like it was no big deal. Then she blurted out that for twelve-hundred dollars she could handle the case. But first, she needed some background information about me.

She asked me, had I ever been arrested before, and I responded, "No, of course no." She stared at me with this all-knowing eye and replied with a smirk on her face, "It's all right, you can tell me, even though your father's here, you can tell me if you have been arrested before. Come on!"

I was furious and ready to leave. What kind of help was she going to give me when she just assumed I had a police record and she didn't believe me. She painted a pretty bleak scenario of my chances of beating this assault charge. She said my best possible hope was to plead guilty and receive a suspended sentence.

As I sat in that chair, my mind filled with every graphic image of prison life. Every prison movie, prison documentary and prison story I had ever seen or heard blanketed my thoughts and sent absolute horror and fear to my heart.

I think at that point, everybody in the room was thinking the same thing, because they all just looked at me. I was afraid to ask. I feared what she might say but I had to know.

TEDDY: Am I going to jail for this?

WOMAN LAWYER *(No emotion)*: Yes, it's quite possible. Yes, it's possible.

TEDDY: I don't think I heard anything else after that. Here I was thinking that I was embarking upon the trail of vindication and justice. And they were about to send me on the express-way to Lorton Prison. What the hell happened to innocent till proven guilty? This was more like guilty till proven guiltier.

Less than five minutes of horror was turning into a never-ending nightmare. A nightmare so terrifying that no matter how much I screamed, I couldn't wake from.

(Teddy then remembers meeting Edelstein, a new lawyer in Washington.

David Alexander, David Jr. and Teddy are at table watching film David Jr. took of beating. The brief film is very dark with violent sounds of Teddy's screams.)

SUZANNE:

Dear Governor Wilder:

I've received replies from the police chief, senators and county manager. I have a new list. But why should we have to defend ourselves with letters of character when we are innocent? All our lives we have tried to fit in American society and improve our society.

I've had two letters from Senator Robb.

My son said the D.A. said to him he seems nice but how can she be sure. He says she's a white woman with ruffled blouses.

I have photos of Teddy when he was president of the African-American students group at Riverdale and his speeches. I send them to you.

I keep dreaming of suffocation.

The next day. Cleveland. Greenroom, Ohio Theatre.
Rehearsals of Suzanne's play The Ohio State Murders. *The*
P.A. system is on, and muffled dialogue from the stage can
be heard. Again Suzanne is writing letters. And she has not
taken off her coat and scarf.

SUZANNE:

Dear Governor Wilder:

Teddy won't tell me what happens when he goes to
Washington.

What did I do? he screamed.

Yesterday I took the bus to Yellow Springs to Teddy's
rehearsal at Antioch.

I've written you before about my son and my street
in New York City where I live.

At this moment, I am in Cleveland rehearsing *The
Ohio State Murders.*

*(Suzanne is interrupted by the P.A. system from the stage,
which broadcasts parts of her play, read by the play's Heroine.)*

HEROINE'S VOICE: I was asked to talk about the violent imagery in my work: bloodied heads, severed limbs, dead father, dead Nazis, dying Jesus. The chairman said, we do want to hear about your brief years here at Ohio State but we also want you to talk about the violent imagery in your stories and plays. When I visited Ohio State last year it struck me as a series of desperate dark landscapes just as it had in 1949, the autumn of my freshman year.

I used to write down locations in order to learn the campus: the Oval, behind the green, the golf hut, behind Zoology. The tennis courts beyond the golf hut, the Olentangy River, the stadium off to the right, the main library at the head of the Oval. The old Union across from the dorm, High Street at the end of the path, downtown Columbus, the Deshler Wallach, Lazarus, the train station. The geography made me anxious.

The zigzagged streets beyond the Oval were regions of law, medicine, Mirror Lake, the Greek theatre, the lawn behind the dorm where the white girls sunned. The ravine which would be the scene of the murder and Mrs. Tyler's boarding house in the Negro district.

The music I remembered most was a song called "Don't Go Away Mad," and the music from *A Place in the Sun,* that movie with Elizabeth Taylor and Montgomery Clift based on Theodore Dreiser's *American Tragedy.*

(Suzanne continues letter to Governor Wilder.)

SUZANNE *(Writing)*:

When I'm in Cleveland, I think of New York. In the foyers of the brownstones on my street people are robbed just as darkness comes. One man carried an ax and a gun at four o'clock in the afternoon. The next

morning at fifteen past eight I leave the apartment to go
to class at New York University.

*(Scene: Morning at fifteen past eight Suzanne leaves apart-
ment to go to class at New York University. Waiting for her,
sitting on the stoop, is a Woman her age searching for food
in the garbage. Woman stops Suzanne.)*

WOMAN: I want to warn you that there is a vault underneath the
street where brimstone lies and over it gunpowder. There is
a plan for muggers on the Upper West Side to come up
through a trapdoor dressed like workmen, cast holes into
the vault so that it catches fire and consumes all. I know
everyone.

*(Suzanne walks toward Broadway. And looks back. The
Woman is drinking from a paper cup she picks up from the
curb. She waves at Suzanne.)*

SUZANNE: My lecture that morning at New York University in
the Tisch School of the Arts was to be "The Construction of
a Play with Aristotelian Elements."

(Pause. Fade.)

===

SUZANNE: I wonder where the policeman lives. Teddy would
only say he has black hair. You mustn't think of how he
looks, Mom. I'm quite worried my letters of character are
being intercepted. The precious letters I've spent time
gathering for my son's defense.

(As Suzanne's speech fades, the lights come up on Antioch.
Teddy at rehearsal watching Student Actor on stage. As
Actor speaks, Teddy holds police manual which is on the
table. Student Actor looks through manual.)

STUDENT ACTOR: This is what they teach at the police academy?
This is the police manual?

(Teddy nods. Rehearsal stops.
Student Actor reads fragment of manual. Cast stares at
Teddy.)

STUDENT ACTOR:

Blacks: Asking "personal questions" of someone one has
met for the first time is seen as improper and intrusive.

Whites: Inquiring about jobs, family, etc., of someone one
has met for the first time is seen as friendly.

Blacks: Use of direct questions is sometimes seen as
harassment, e.g., asking when something will be fin-
ished is seen as rushing that person to finish.

Whites: Use of direct questions for personal information is
permissible.

Blacks: "Breaking in" during conversation is usually toler-
ated. Competition for the floor is granted to the person
who is most assertive.

Whites: Rules of turn-taking in conversation dictate that
one person has the floor at a time until all his points are
made.

Blacks: Public acting up especially when confronted by
authority.

Whites: Respect for authority.

(Teddy listens to Student Actor; then he hears Unseen
Questioner's voice as he thinks.)

UNSEEN QUESTIONER: How long did you find yourself in the position of losing some consciousness?

TEDDY: Just a matter of seconds from the time that he struck me to the time I went to the ground and just that time period.

UNSEEN QUESTIONER: That's all?

TEDDY: Yes.

UNSEEN QUESTIONER: Counsel asked you questions regarding your reputation. Do you recall those questions?

TEDDY: Yes.

UNSEEN QUESTIONER: All right. Prior to the incident in question, on January 11, did you have a criminal record?

TEDDY: No. *(Fade)*

(Lights up on Ohio Theatre greenroom.)

SUZANNE:

Dear Atty Edelstein:

You say I must see Teddy's case realistically. Few people win cases against the police; the judge tends to side with them. And you are doing everything possible that I must understand it is your profession to prosecute the police and you hope I won't write too many letters. I've heard you're brilliant at prosecuting the police but I keep asking will Teddy have to go to jail. And you said that's a possibility. Everything is a possibility. But what about the videotape?

EDELSTEIN'S VOICE: Mrs. Alexander, the videotape is dark and it has only the very end of the incident. You must get hold of your emotions. I do think in the end it will come out fairly. But I don't know if it will come out fairly without a long process. I've prosecuted many policemen. Prepare yourself for this case going to trial by jury.

SUZANNE: And then the jury will be white Southerners?

(The stage at Antioch becomes visible; Student Actor speaks inaudibly. Teddy watches. Members of the Student Cast sit with him at the table. Student Cast start to read from manual.)

STUDENT CAST:

   Blacks: Hats and sunglasses are sometimes considered as adornments, much like jewelry, to be worn inside.

   Whites: Clothing is utilitarian, thus hats and sunglasses are considered as outerwear and are to be removed indoors.

   Blacks: Touching of one's hair by another person is often considered as offensive.

   Whites: Touching of one's hair by another person is a sign of affection.

   Blacks: Direct eye contact in conversation, thus "rolling one's eyes" is considered offensive.

   Whites: Direct eye contact is considered to be a sign of attentiveness and respect.

   Blacks: Public behavior, e.g., at a play or concert is emotionally intense, dynamic and demonstrative, as in laughter, shouts, etc.

   Whites: Public behavior is characterized as modest and emotionally restrained. Outward displays are seen as irresponsible or in bad taste.

   Blacks: Common use of threats to gain respect and fear from others.

   Whites: Posture is "Do not make threats unless you are prepared to carry them out."

   Blacks: Clear distinction between "argument" and "fight." Verbal abuse is not necessarily a precursor to violence.

   Whites: Heated arguments are viewed as suggesting that violence is imminent. *(Silence. They stare at Teddy)*

(In the Ohio Theatre Suzanne writes.)

SUZANNE:

Dear State Senator:

I dream of March wandering in the Palo Alto hills when a soldier attempts to murder him, piercing his face with a poniard and breaking some of his teeth. Then students appear in white tennis outfits. Behind them, Patrice. They take her to the Quad where she is condemned to stand naked.

Are you aware of all the hungry, homeless men walking the cross blocks 86th, 87th, 88th from Broadway to Riverside Drive?

My son, Teddy, won't tell me about his meetings with his lawyer, the district attorney, the police chief. But he did tell me about his father's session with the lawyer again.

——

(Pretrial deposition. One of many white lawyers with the prosecution.

David Alexander is seen; Lawyer's voice is heard.)

DAVID ALEXANDER: I saw this officer with a drawn gun, yes.

LAWYER: And did any of them say that they had seen an officer with a drawn gun?

DAVID ALEXANDER: I don't think so. I'm not sure.

LAWYER: Didn't they say they didn't?

DAVID ALEXANDER: I'm not sure. I'm not sure.

LAWYER: What did the officer do with this drawn gun?

DAVID ALEXANDER: Well, the officer had the gun drawn and then someone said, "Stay back."

And then I heard my son yell out, "Dad." At that point, frankly, at that point, I moved over in that direction.

LAWYER: Did you ever ask your son, or could you tell, how he knew you were there, when he yelled, "Dad"?

DAVID ALEXANDER: He yelled, "Dad." I don't know.

LAWYER: What position was he in when he yelled, "Dad"?

DAVID ALEXANDER: At that point, I think he was over—he was almost—I'm not sure whether he was over the vehicle, like that *(Indicating)* with his head turned.

LAWYER: Excuse me. Could you use words to describe what you're doing physically?

DAVID ALEXANDER: When he yelled, "Dad," I walked on past this officer, and walked over to the area where he was on the car. I'm not sure whether he was face down, and his head was turned, like that, but he yelled, "Dad."

That's when I walked over there, and at that point, they were doing something to him, and I said, you know, "Stop shaking him," or "Why are you shaking him?"

LAWYER: Who was shaking him?

DAVID ALEXANDER: The two officers.

LAWYER: Can you describe them?

DAVID ALEXANDER: No, I cannot describe them.

LAWYER: Were they in uniform?

DAVID ALEXANDER: They were in uniform. As far as I know, yes, they were in uniform.

LAWYER: Did they have nameplates on their uniforms?

DAVID ALEXANDER: I couldn't see the nameplates, if they had them. I don't know.

LAWYER: Can you describe whether they were tall or short, white or black, fat or skinny?

DAVID ALEXANDER: No, because they were standing there and—I couldn't describe them.

LAWYER: Were you facing Teddy's back, or were you looking right at Teddy's face when this was occurring?

DAVID ALEXANDER: Well, I was at an angle, so I was seeing his back and his head turned.

LAWYER: How far away were you, from where Teddy was, at that time?

DAVID ALEXANDER: Well, it's a matter of feet. I don't know whether it was ten feet, but it wasn't very far.

LAWYER: Where were you standing, in either the yard, or the driveway?

DAVID ALEXANDER: I was still in the yard.

LAWYER: Near what? What portion of the yard?

DAVID ALEXANDER: Toward the front left of the yard.

LAWYER: Where would that be in relation to the driveway?

DAVID ALEXANDER: Our driveway is adjacent, so it would have been in front, left part of the yard, then the driveway, immediately to my left.

LAWYER: Did any of the officers say anything to you when—?

DAVID ALEXANDER: No, they didn't. I kept saying—I kept trying to get someone's attention. It was like chaos. It was chaotic. I'm saying, "Hello, hello. Wait a minute." I'm trying to get somebody's attention. I couldn't get anybody's attention, so I called out any number of times, and even said, "Look, you know, I live here. What's going on," or "Hey, look, look, listen." I'm trying to get somebody's attention. I got no one's attention.

LAWYER: Have you ever been the victim of an assault?

DAVID ALEXANDER: No.

LAWYER: I notice you're missing the tips of two of your fingers.

DAVID ALEXANDER: Yes.

LAWYER: How did that occur?

DAVID ALEXANDER: I was sixteen years old, working in a steel mill. A steel grinder fell on them and broke them, cut them off.

LAWYER: Where was this?

DAVID ALEXANDER: That was in Franklin, Ohio, where I grew up.

LAWYER: Have you ever had any unpleasant experiences with police officers, prior to that evening?

DAVID ALEXANDER: Yes. *(Fade)*

(Lights come up; Lawyer and David Alexander continue.)

LAWYER: What happened next?

DAVID ALEXANDER: Well, then Teddy came out, and we left and went to the hospital.

LAWYER: Was there anything unusual about Teddy's physical appearance, when he came out—?

DAVID ALEXANDER: Yes, his face was swollen. There was mud and dirt on his face. His jacket was torn, and his pants were muddy where he had been dragged across the driveway. Yes. He looked terrible.

LAWYER: Could you describe the jacket that you said was torn?

DAVID ALEXANDER: No, I don't remember the type of jacket, but it was torn.

LAWYER: What became of the jacket?

DAVID ALEXANDER: I have it at home.

LAWYER: Where was it torn?

DAVID ALEXANDER: The details I don't know. I just know it was torn and he was muddy.

LAWYER: What part of his face was puffed or swollen?

DAVID ALEXANDER: His eyes and his cheek.

LAWYER: Which one?

DAVID ALEXANDER: This one.

LAWYER: Which side? You're indicating the left side? Did he have any cuts on his body that you could see?

DAVID ALEXANDER: Well, his face was bruised, and of course he did have his clothes on. He had his jacket on, so at that point, no.

LAWYER: Did you see any cuts on his face?

DAVID ALEXANDER: No, just mud on his face, and on his jacket, and on his trousers. Then we went to the hospital. One of the attendants came out and said, "Oh, he's pretty well beaten up." And then we waited and we waited and finally I went back and saw Teddy and he'd had some examinations, and he was laying on the bed, beaten up.

And then the doctor came. Another doctor came and said, "We want to take some more examinations," so they took him back and they took some more examinations.

LAWYER: Was any of this filmed by your son?

(Fade.)

======

(Lights up on greenroom.)

SUZANNE *(Writing)*:
    To the President of the NAACP:
        I've written you before about my son, Teddy.
        On the bus from Dayton to Cleveland I dream I see . . . Teddy in Attorney Edelstein's office on M Street in Washington.

DREAM SCENE: *(Teddy is sitting in Attorney Edelstein's office on M Street in Washington.)*

TEDDY: I'm finishing up my term papers in Washington because on campus the plague is increasing lawlessness on the Ohio border. And none of the students are allowed to have meat during Lent.

    I want to study in Cleveland but Cleveland is submerged in Dale Creek.

SUZANNE *(Writing)*:
    A creek that ran through my old neighborhood.

TEDDY: I've discovered that after World War II moths called Canadian Soldiers covered the shores of Lake Erie one July evening and that bit by bit that section of the city sank into the creek. If you want to see your father and brother again all we have to do, Mom, is walk to 88th and St. Clair Park (now called Martin Luther King) and we will see your old neighborhood just as it was.

(Fade.)

SUZANNE *(Writing)*:
     And when Teddy was on the submerged street yesterday he said he saw my father mowing the lawn in 1943, hurrying so he wouldn't be late for the Cleveland Indians game.
     My father didn't get home until late because after the game he went to a meeting of the NAACP.

TEDDY: I saw your grandmother. Remember, she took care of you and your brother the fall of 1941 because your mother worked in a war plant. She was planting petunias in the tree lawn.

SUZANNE *(Writing)*:
     We were all members of the NAACP. Can you help?

(Suzanne sits in the greenroom; Teddy, making a call, is seen in his room at Antioch.
     Phone rings in greenroom.)

SUZANNE: Teddy, what happened in Washington yesterday? I can come to Antioch on the bus.
     I can't stop thinking of the Ghost in *Hamlet*, his large head, slimy dried blood oozing from his skin.

". . . Sleeping within my orchard,
My custom always of the afternoon,
Upon my secure hour thy uncle stole
With juice of cursed verbena in a vial
And in the porches of my ear did pour
The leprous distillment, whose effect
Holds such an enmity with blood of man. . . ."

(As Suzanne speaks, Teddy thinks: Unseen Questioner has him on the hood of the police car.)

TEDDY: The officer was pushing me on top of the car and because I had been kicked in the chest I had a very difficult time breathing and I asked the officer very politely—I said, "Sir, I can't breathe," I said, "I'm an American citizen, could you please let me up and breathe?"

UNSEEN QUESTIONER: What officer was that?

TEDDY: My face is face down on the car. I could not see who—what officer it was.

UNSEEN QUESTIONER: Do you know from talking with your relatives who the officer was that you addressed?

TEDDY: No. The—I then—instead of having him—I felt like I was going to pass out because my chest was on the hood of the car I was having a difficult time breathing and I tried to raise up a couple of inches to get some air in my lungs and at that point I was struck on the side—in my left side and I yelled out.

UNSEEN QUESTIONER: Who struck you?

(Fade.)

SUZANNE: What happened in Washington?

TEDDY: I met with a woman called Wagner. She's . . . Assistant D.A.

I also met with the district attorney. The prosecution knows my defense but we know nothing of what they will say, Edelstein says they probably have a surprise.

SUZANNE: You mean they know all your information and you know little of theirs?

TEDDY: Yes, Mom, I may have to go to jail. They want me to plea-bargain.

SUZANNE: I've made a list of mothers whose sons have been beaten by the police. I haven't heard from the governor yet.

TEDDY: You know by now the governor doesn't get involved in these cases.

SUZANNE: But I must talk to him. My friend Charles called. When he was just out of college he worked briefly as a detective. I asked him about the number of letters. "You're supposed to write a few letters, Suzanne. I called to give you the name of a scholar on prosecuting the police as well as another lawyer I know who does legal aid as well as a public defender in Brooklyn. You must try and talk to all of them. You need all this information so you can judge what your lawyer is doing."

(Pause)

Teddy, are you going to the group for victims of violent crime?

TEDDY: Mom, I may have to go to jail.

(Silence)

Tell me about the times Uncle March disappeared before. You think he may have gone to Ghana. Where in Ghana?

(Fade.)

———

(In the greenroom later that night. Suzanne writes to her daughter, Patrice.)

SUZANNE:

Dear Patrice,

I can tell Edelstein thinks I may jeopardize Teddy's case by writing too many letters. He told me to write two: one to the governor and one to the county manager. I have written seventeen, but I haven't told him.

I begged him to tell me about the detective he said he uses. I asked him was it possible for me to talk to the detective. I wanted to find out where the policeman lives. I wanted to see the policeman who dragged my son in the mud.

I could tell Edelstein had begged Teddy not to tell me too many details.

"You're too emotional, Mrs. Alexander," he said, as we walked through his glass offices. He said he's afraid I may do something foolish. He judged me for being a mother. "I'm sorry I cried in your glass offices," I said.

Patrice, whatever happened about the detective who was supposed to investigate the policeman and his past? He must have found something. This policeman must have beat other people. There's no place I can go and get that information.

Dear Governor Wilder:

This is my final telegram to you. I'm still in Cleveland rehearsing my play about my years at Ohio State. Every day when I come to the Ohio Theatre I think of my father and brother. I pass their graves in Lakeview Cemetery.

I also think of my brother-in-law, March Alexander. I'm sure you've heard of him, Professor Emeritus at Stanford. He lives in a cottage by Lake Lagunita on the campus. He vanished again last week through the arch of eucalyptus trees, vanished. His depression about the conditions of African-Americans has worsened. Sometimes he sits in the sun near the Leland Stanford Chapel. (Stanford offers him economic security for life) yet the columns of the Quad, the golf course, the Palo Alto hills have become a source of melancholy to him. I know you must remember he was one of the first blacks to go to Africa to live. Now he has many illnesses.

I seek your help once more because my daughter Patrice (a lecturer at Stanford) called. She said Teddy told her not to tell me but the district attorney said Teddy may be denied the trial with judge. And we will have to wait several months for a trial by jury and Teddy said they know we fear a trial by jury. Juries tend to side with the police and the police would be sure to have secret witnesses. I have written to the county manager, the police chief, the NAACP. Can you help my son?

(Fade.)

═══

(A few hours later. Night in the greenroom.)

SUZANNE *(Narrates Dream Scene)*: In my dream the commander held the intercepted letters, reading them aloud to show me they were in his possession.

DREAM SCENE: *(A "commander" holds up intercepted letters, reading silently.)*

SUZANNE: Please show them to the assistant district attorney so that she will be sympathetic to my son. I'm praying you will. I pray every day on my knees in my mother's guest room, kneeling by the old secretary with my brother's baby shoes on the top shelf.

DREAM SCENE: *(Suzanne on knees.)*

SUZANNE: I miss rehearsals, rise in the night to pray. I get on my knees and pray for Teddy.

DREAM SCENE: *(Suzanne praying on knees.)*

SUZANNE: You're brave. No matter what you say, I see the fear in your eyes.
    "Is the legal system fair?" I ask Edelstein again on the phone.
    "How many cases has Edelstein won against the police?" I ask Patrice.
    "I don't know how to get that information, Mom. We have to trust him."
    "But he's a stranger."

(Fade.)

===

(Lights up on Teddy in his room at Antioch. Suzanne calls him.)

SUZANNE: Teddy did you talk to the lawyer today? . . . Are you going to the campus group for battered victims? I'm sending Governor Wilder another message.
TEDDY: I can't talk tonight, Mom. My head hurts.

There may not be a trial by judge. The prosecution wants to take this to trial by jury.

There may not be a need for you to come to Washington.

SUZANNE: I don't understand.

But I want to be there.

TEDDY: The prosecution wants the trial to go to trial by jury. There may not be a trial next week. The prosecution still wants me to say I struck the policeman. If I do I'll get two months probation and the record will be wiped clean.

SUZANNE: I don't understand.

TEDDY: I'm not going to confess to anything I didn't do. My head hurts.

There may not be a trial. But I'm going to Washington in an hour.

(Student Cast is onstage, they are silent. Teddy remembers charges not being dropped.

He remembers actual scene: Mr. Edelstein and Teddy in Ms. Wagner's office.)

MS. WAGNER: So why did you want this meeting?

MR. EDELSTEIN: I wanted the opportunity to discuss my client's situation and to see if we could amicably resolve this matter.

MS. WAGNER: Resolve the matter? Mr. Alexander assaulted an officer. That is a serious offense. And this matter will go to court.

MR. EDELSTEIN: My client did not assault the officer and that is why we have come to you, so that you could hear my client's side of the story.

MS. WAGNER: Mr. Edelstein, your client's story is of no interest to me. Officer Holzer pursued your client for three blocks with his lights and siren on and then chased him down a dead-end street. Mr. Alexander was belligerent and hostile

and then assaulted Officer Holzer. The charge is clear-cut
and we are very confident that the court will return a guilty
verdict on Mr. Alexander. So if there is nothing further, I am
very busy.

MR. EDELSTEIN: I appreciate your position, but I have two witnesses who saw Officer Holzer beat my client without
provocation. I think it would be in the best interest of all
those involved to resolve this matter prior to trial.

MS. WAGNER: We will see you in court, Mr. Edelstein. I am busy,
thank you.

(Fade.)

=====

*(Lights up on Suzanne reading in her mother's house; desk
with her brother's baby shoes.)*

SUZANNE:

Dear Mom,

When I called Edelstein he explained to me that he
was contacted by the district attorney's office and they
told him they were going to present a motion to the district court judge to have the case heard directly before
a jury versus the usual first step of before a judge. He
says we should grant no interviews to the press even
though the *Washington Post* and the *Times* have contacted him. He said even if we lost in front of a judge
we could get a second chance before a jury but by by-
passing the judge the D.A. hopes to convict Teddy in
one shot. Juries in the eastern district of Virginia tend
to side with the police. The letters have infuriated
them. And they're going to teach us a lesson.

Love,
Patrice

PATRICE'S VOICE: Mom, Teddy never told you about the time
    when he was in L.A. when he and our cousin got lost and
    they tried to ask some officers for directions. They pulled
    them out of the car. They were almost killed underneath
    that dark underpass near Denny's.

(Fade.)

Hotel. Washington. Early morning.
Day there may not be a trial.

SUZANNE *(Narrates Dream Scene)*: I dream Governor Wilder answers my letters. Enclosed is a thesis on the force and effect of firing all manual weapons and another thesis on present remedies against the plague and the play *Hamlet*.

I'm sitting with the Antioch students in the snow on the Quad; beyond, some play football, and we go to Yorick's grave.

DREAM SCENE: *(Suzanne is sitting with Antioch students in the snow on the Quad; beyond some play football. She sleepwalks toward Yorick's grave. March enters.*

Suzanne sees Teddy standing in Yorick's grave being questioned.)

SUZANNE *(Continues narrating Dream Scene)*: I am sleepwalking toward Yorick's grave. March enters our room in Earl's Court the Autumn of 1961. We arrive in London from

Southampton on the way to Ghana, there is some problem with a visa.

DREAM SCENE: *(Suzanne sees Teddy standing in Yorick's grave being questioned.)*

UNSEEN QUESTIONER: Now, when you went to the hospital after leaving the—you went to the emergency room at National Orthopedic Hospital after leaving the detention center, what problems—medical problems were you having when you went in there?

TEDDY: I had—I was having difficulty breathing. I had bruises on my face that were painful. I had lacer—cuts, lacerations on both of my wrists.

I had my back, or my lower back and my upper back and my stomach were—I was in extreme pain on both sides of my body. And I had several cuts on my lip and inside my mouth. *(Indicating)*

DREAM SCENE: *(Teddy standing in Yorick's grave.)*

UNSEEN QUESTIONER: What treatment did they give you at the emergency room?

TEDDY: They gave me a physical, and then they checked—they gave me X rays to see if there were any broken bones.

UNSEEN QUESTIONER: And what did the X rays show?

SUZANNE *(Continues narrating Dream Scene)*: I dream of a summer evening in Cleveland in the 1940s. My father and his friends held the meeting of the NAACP on an old campsite I loved as a child, a place called Aurora, Ohio.

I walked down a path lined with whitewashed stones. But seeing into the wooden cabin where my father and his friends sat was difficult. The Canadian Soldier moths covered the screened door of the cabin. It was Cabin 17.

DREAM SCENE: *(Suzanne walks down a path lined with whitewashed stones. Seeing into the wooden cabin where her father and his friends are is difficult. Canadian Soldier moths cover the screen door of the cabin, Cabin 17. Suzanne writes Cabin 17 down on a yellow pad. And stands on bottom step. She hears her father and his friends laughing. She hears her father whistle, "Let Me Call You Sweetheart.")*

SUZANNE *(Continues narrating Dream Scene)*: I'll come back in August when the Canadian Soldiers die. I want to see my father and his friends. I hope when I return to Cabin 17 in August I will hear my father discuss (as they always did) how to make Cleveland a better place for Negroes, how to raise money for the Quincy Library and for the cornerstone ceremony for the Central Y and, as they always did, talk about justice for the children, and Bob Feller.

Teddy, was the back porch of my house with the trellis of honeysuckle submerged there on the floor of Dale Creek?

TEDDY: Yes. I saw your mother sitting on the steps stirring a cake and you were seven and licking vanilla icing.

(Sounds of father's friends singing. Fade.)

═══

(Phone. Teddy appears. He is dressed in a suit.)

SUZANNE: Patrice called. Your Uncle March's back. She says he's dazed but fine. A Mr. Chavez brought him in a Buick. He was with a group of migrant workers near Palo Alto.

TEDDY: Mom, I'm happy.

(Pause)

There may not be a trial today but we're prepared and we're going to court.

I want you to stay in the hotel. I'll call you as soon as I can.

(Fade.
Suzanne sits motionless, image of Yorick's grave before her.)

TEDDY: Edelstein expected the proceedings to last several minutes while the judge granted the motion. But the D.A.'s plan
began to unravel.

My case was called and the assistant commonwealth
attorney explained to the judge, the Honorable Cartwright,
why the case should not be heard in front of her and taken
to jury.

The judge disagreed with Wagner and denied her
motion. The case would be heard today by her.

*(Fade to trial. Courtroom. In the courtroom are Teddy, Mr.
Edelstein, the Judge, Ms. Wagner and the court reporter.
Teddy sits separately.)*

JUDGE: Let's proceed with the opening statements.
MS. WAGNER: Yes, Your Honor. May it please the court, the commonwealth's chief witness to testify is Officer Holzer. He
will tell this court that in the early morning of January 11th,
he was traveling in his police cruiser on a routine patrol.
On that morning, he was traveling westbound on Columbia
Pike when he noticed a car with a taillight not working
properly. At that point, the officer made a decision to effec-
tuate a routine traffic stop.

The officer falls in behind the car, which makes a right
onto Monroe. The officer decides to enact his lights, his
emergency lights to make his presence known to the defendant. But the defendant does not stop. He continues to
drive another block up Monroe. The officer's lights now
have continued to blaze. And it's dark out in a residential
neighborhood at this point.

The officer then sees the driver make a left onto Riverdale. Still the defendant does not stop. The officer at this point is alone at two o'clock in the morning in a side street that happens to be a dead end that goes into a park. And still, the defendant continues to drive very slowly, not responding to the presence of the officer with his emergency equipment activated. And at this point now, a siren has gone off. The defendant, not stopping, turns the car into the driveway of a home and gets out of the car. Officer Holzer says to the defendant, "Sir, get back in your car." The defendant does not do that.

(Light remains on Suzanne sitting motionless, Yorick's grave before her.)

MS. WAGNER: He says again, "Sir, get back in your car." The defendant will not do that. And he says to the officer, "I don't have to get back in my car. What is it that you want?" Your Honor, the officer has now encountered a hostile citizen.

At this point, since Mr. Alexander will not get into the car, the officer says to him, "All right, then come over here." At this time, Mr. Alexander approached the officer. The defendant was wearing a large parka that was bulky. He could not see his hands clearly and he did not know what was in his pockets. The officer is in a state of heightened awareness because he had now just pursued this man through three blocks in the middle of the night to a dead-end street not knowing what is going on. The officer then approaches the defendant, telling him that he is about to pat him down. It is at that critical point that the defendant struck the police officer. Once the defendant struck Officer Holzer, the officer responded in the only manner which he could to ensure his welfare and to make sure nothing else more serious happened.

And what happens next, Your Honor, is the defendant

continued to resist. He scuffled and fought with the officer for numerous minutes. The defendant was then finally, after backup arrived, was finally subdued, handcuffed, taken to the police department and during the course of the struggle, he was struck several times by the police officer.

(Teddy sits separately, motionless.)

MS. WAGNER: This man struck the police officer and the mere fact that if, indeed, the officer ended up besting this man at the end of that confrontation does not vitiate the fact that this man struck the police officer, committing an assault and battery. And we're going to ask the court to find him guilty of that at the close of evidence.

JUDGE: Mr. Edelstein.

MR. EDELSTEIN: Yes, Your Honor, what we're going to show is, if we have to, that no assault was committed by this man on Officer Holzer. What the evidence is really going to show, in fact, I was struck by counsel's remarks here, is that officer Holzer bested, if you will, Mr. Alexander. The short of it is, he beat him up. The evidence will show, Your Honor, that Mr. Alexander realized he was in his residence. Obviously, he was going home. He got out of his car and asked the officer politely what he wanted. The officer told him to get back in the car. Mr. Alexander said, "Look, it's my house." The officer again—

(Trial fades.)

———

(Lights on Teddy. He remembers this scene:)

UNSEEN QUESTIONER: How long did you find yourself in the position of losing some consciousness?

TEDDY: Just a matter of seconds from the time that he struck me to the time I went to the ground.

UNSEEN QUESTIONER: That's all?

TEDDY: Yes.

UNSEEN QUESTIONER: Isn't it really true that you tried to flee the area and when you were caught you viciously attacked Officer Holzer?

TEDDY: No, no. Never. I'm afraid of the police.

UNSEEN QUESTIONER: Afraid of the police?

TEDDY: I would never hit a police officer I . . . the nightmares.

(Teddy remembers: He is sitting in a passenger's side of a car with another black man in the driver's seat. A white Officer has his gun in Teddy's face. The Officer is nervous and his gun hand is shaking.)

OFFICER: You were moving erratically in the car. Were you trying to hide something?

TEDDY: Officer, we were listening to the radio.

OFFICER: What were you hiding? Do you have any automatic weapons or drugs in the car?

TEDDY: No.

OFFICER: Get out of the car and keep your hands up while I search the car.

(Fade. Light dims.)

———

(Trial progresses.)

MR. EDELSTEIN: —said, "Get back in the car." Mr. Alexander then went to the rear of the car, where the officer had asked him to come. The evidence will show, Your Honor, that the officer confronted him.

Mr. Alexander didn't touch him, didn't put his hand on him, didn't do a thing. The officer grabbed him and then hit him. Mr. Alexander was hit and he'll testify he was hit so hard he was stunned and knocked to the ground. Officer Holzer grabbed him, dragged him across the parking area there, this is all on private property, Your Honor, and kicked him and beat him severely many, many times. He was beaten quite badly, Your Honor, and finally handcuffed by Officer Holzer. Your Honor, he offered no resistance. Your Honor, Officer Holzer at some point had summoned backup officers. They appeared. Mr. Alexander was placed in handcuffs and then placed spread-eagle on the front of a police vehicle and injured further.

Your Honor, this man was beaten without provocation. This is allegedly a trial of Mr. Alexander for assault on a police officer. We think that the charge simply doesn't apply here.

Here's a man confronted by a police officer in his own front yard and as the evidence will show, beaten by that officer. And we think there's no credible evidence which the state can offer that will convince Your Honor to find beyond a reasonable doubt that this man is guilty of an assault. Thank you.

JUDGE: Thank you.

MS. WAGNER: We call Officer Holzer.

(Officer Holzer comes into the courtroom.)

MS. WAGNER: Please state your name for the court.

OFFICER HOLZER: Thomas Holzer.

MS. WAGNER: And how are you currently employed?

OFFICER HOLZER: I am a special agent with U.S. Secret Service.

MS. WAGNER: And before you were a special agent, where did you work?

OFFICER HOLZER: With Arlington County as a police officer for
     three years.
MS. WAGNER: When did you start your new job?
OFFICER HOLZER: This past Monday.
MS. WAGNER: Could you tell us what specifically happened at
     around 2:00 A.M. January 11th?
OFFICER HOLZER: I was westbound on Columbia Pike when I
     noticed Mr. Alexander's car in front of me.

(Trial fades.)

                         .   ===

(Lights on Teddy. He remembers:)

SUZANNE: Teddy, are you going to the group for victims of vio-
     lent crime?
TEDDY: Mom, I may have to go to jail. I'm scared, Mom. There
     are things I haven't told you. . . . About California.

*(He remembers. Teddy and his Cousin are in a car slowly
driving. It is dark.)*

TEDDY: I think we're close. Where the hell is the entrance to the
     freeway?
COUSIN: Let's go back to Denny's and try again.
TEDDY: Wait a minute. I see a police car behind us. I'll ask them
     for help.

*(The car stops under an underpass. Two white police officers
in an L.A.P.D. police car rush toward Teddy and his Cousin.)*

OFFICER *(Yelling)*: Get the fuck out of the car niggers.

(The officers pull Teddy and his Cousin out of the car and throw them against the wall.)

OFFICER: Assume the position.

TEDDY: What's going on?

OFFICER: Shut up nigger. What are you doing in this part of town?

TEDDY: I . . .

(The Officer pulls out his gun and places it against Teddy's temple.)

OFFICER: Nigger, I'll blow your head off. Where did you get the Jaguar?

TEDDY: It's my cousin's, Isaac Alexander. He lives in Beverly Hills.

(The Officer violently body searches Teddy. He grabs him under his testicles and in the crevice of his buttocks several times.)

OFFICER: Beverly Hills? You niggers better not be lying.

(The other officer pulls out his gun.
Fade.)

=====

(Trial continues.)

MS. WAGNER: What happened next?

OFFICER HOLZER: I noticed that there was one small red light in the rear section. I pulled behind it and followed it. The vehicle turned right on Monroe and I continued to follow.

MS. WAGNER: And what did you do?

OFFICER HOLZER: I followed it until it got to the intersection of Riverdale. At that point I attempted to stop it for a traffic violation and put my emergency lights on, and the vehicle responded by turning left on Riverdale. And I followed it.

MS. WAGNER: Did the car stop?

OFFICER HOLZER: No, it did not.

MS. WAGNER: Then what happened?

OFFICER HOLZER: I continued to follow, then I turned on my siren and he still didn't stop. He continued all the way down the dead-end street. The car swung into the driveway and the driver stepped out of the car quickly and started walking toward the house.

MS. WAGNER: What happened then?

OFFICER HOLZER: When people quickly get out of the car like that, I think they are trying to flee. So I jumped out of my car immediately.

MS. WAGNER: Were you concerned for your safety?

OFFICER HOLZER: Yes. I was fearful at the time. I was alarmed because he failed to stop and I was alone and it was a dark street. I decided to try and give him some directions verbally until I had time to get on the radio and ask for another unit.

MS. WAGNER: And you gave the defendant directions?

OFFICER HOLZER: Yes, I said, "Sir, please get back into your car."

MS. WAGNER: And what did he say?

OFFICER HOLZER: He yelled back at me, "This is my house." I asked him again to get back into the car. I said, "This is a . . .

(Trial fades.)

═══

(Lights on Teddy thinking.)

TEDDY: I pulled the car latch and began to open the door. And before I could open the door all the way, Officer Holzer had made his way to the back of the Granada. He said, "Come back here."

UNSEEN QUESTIONER: What did you say?

TEDDY: I closed the door and I made my way to the back of the car.

UNSEEN QUESTIONER: Did you say anything?

TEDDY: No.

UNSEEN QUESTIONER: Then what happened?

TEDDY: I got to the back of the car. I was moving very slowly toward him. He was obviously very—he was hostile. So I was concerned. We got   we were—when I got to the end of the car he was standing there and he grabbed my right hand forcibly by the wrist and tried to yank me down. And I pulled my hand away and I said, "Don't touch me."

And at that point he struck me in my face with his hand or with a flashlight and knocked me to the ground.

UNSEEN QUESTIONER: Well, which?

TEDDY: I don't know. It was—it was just a very heavy object. It was either his fist or his flashlight.

UNSEEN QUESTIONER: Couldn't you see?

TEDDY: When I pulled my hand away I was looking to the right. I mean his hand came out, his right hand came and just hit me and I couldn't see it. He basically, I would use the word, sucker punched me.

UNSEEN QUESTIONER: Which hand did he have the flashlight in.

(Fade.)

(Trial resumes.)

OFFICER HOLZER: ". . . traffic stop." He said, "I didn't do any-thing wrong. What did I do?" I said, "This is a traffic stop. Please get back in your car and I'll explain it to you when you're in the car."

MS. WAGNER: Did he get back into the car?

OFFICER HOLZER: No. He said, "You can talk to me here." So I said to Mr. Alexander, okay. I motioned to him with my hands to come back to the rear of his car, and he did. The whole time he was yelling out, verbally violent. He walked up slowly. He had his hands clenched by his waist.

MS. WAGNER: What was he wearing?

OFFICER HOLZER: A parka with pockets in the front. I noticed the pockets were full and bulky. I thought maybe he had a weapon. His manner was very aggressive. He was verbally violent and uncooperative, so I was alarmed. As he walked up, I was watching his hands. I realized his hands were clenched in fists by his waist. Want me to stand up and show you exactly what I mean?

MS. WAGNER: Sure.

OFFICER HOLZER *(Stands up)*: They were down here like this. I was alarmed that his hands were in fists.

MS. WAGNER: So what did you do?

OFFICER HOLZER: I directed him back to the rear of his car and I went to pat him down and in between his fists to see if he had any objects there.

MS. WAGNER: What kind of objects?

OFFICER HOLZER: I was trying to feel for any weapons that he may have on him.

MS. WAGNER: What was his response?

OFFICER HOLZER: His response was to strike me with his right hand to the upper left of my arm approximately where my patch is.

MS. WAGNER: And what did you do?

OFFICER HOLZER: My response was to strike him back in defense. I grabbed him and directed him to the ground to place him in custody.

(In hotel room, Suzanne is motionless.)

MS. WAGNER: What happened as you were trying to place the defendant under arrest?

OFFICER HOLZER: He continued to resist. We struggled and traveled about six to eight feet. I had him on his stomach, but he was still resisting, but I had control as far as he was not moving out of my hold. At that point, I reached for my handcuffs and placed them on the right wrist.

MS. WAGNER: And then what happened?

OFFICER HOLZER: I had to stand up a little to place the cuffs on him. That relieved pressure on Mr. Alexander's back. And at that point he began to resist again. He began to kneel up from the position I had him in and as far as I was concerned, he was resisting my arrest. I was finally able to put the cuffs on.

MS. WAGNER: No further questions.

(Ms. Wagner sits down and Mr. Edelstein gets up.)

MR. EDELSTEIN: When did you see Mr. Alexander's vehicle?

OFFICER HOLZER: I saw it at the 4700 block of Columbia Pike, approximately one block prior to Monroe.

MR. EDELSTEIN: Then how far to Riverdale?

OFFICER HOLZER: About one block.

MR. EDELSTEIN: So you first saw the car with the light burned out on Columbia Pike?

OFFICER HOLZER: Yes.

MR. EDELSTEIN: So you could have stopped that car right there and taken care of the situation?

OFFICER HOLZER: That's correct.

MR. EDELSTEIN: And as the car turned onto Monroe, of course, the same condition existed, right?

OFFICER HOLZER: Yes, but I tend to follow a vehicle to watch for anything else.

MR. EDELSTEIN: Anything else? The car had a burnt-out taillight. There were no further infractions of the law, were there?

OFFICER HOLZER: No.

MR. EDELSTEIN: You saw that there was one black man in the car didn't you?

OFFICER HOLZER: No, I couldn't tell.

MR. EDELSTEIN: You wanted to follow the car, didn't you?

OFFICER HOLZER: Yes, I did.

MR. EDELSTEIN: Because you knew from the very moment you're on Columbia Pike that you could stop that car at any time for its burned-out taillight, correct?

OFFICER HOLZER: I don't believe I had time to stop it on Columbia Pike.

MR. EDELSTEIN: I'm sorry, that wasn't my question. If you'll listen, I'll ask it again.

OFFICER HOLZER: Okay.

MR. EDELSTEIN: You knew from the time you saw the car on Columbia Pike that you could stop it at any time for that burned-out taillight.

OFFICER HOLZER: Right.

MR. EDELSTEIN: And did you turn on your overhead lights on Columbia Pike?

OFFICER HOLZER: No.

MR. EDELSTEIN: Did you sound your siren out there?

OFFICER HOLZER: No, not on Columbia Pike.

MR. EDELSTEIN: Did you turn on your overhead lights as you turned onto Monroe or while you were going up Monroe?

OFFICER HOLZER: No.

MR. EDELSTEIN: Now, did you radio for backup at any point before you reached the Alexander residence?

OFFICER HOLZER: I wished to, but there was interference, so I did not.

MR. EDELSTEIN: Were you armed that night?

OFFICER HOLZER: Yes, I had a nine millimeter.

MR. EDELSTEIN: Any other weapons?

OFFICER HOLZER: A flashlight, a single-handle baton and a canister of mace.

MR. EDELSTEIN: You consider a flashlight a weapon?

OFFICER HOLZER: Yes. We're trained to use it as a weapon.

MR. EDELSTEIN: All right, you saw the car pull into the driveway.

OFFICER HOLZER: Yes.

MR. EDELSTEIN: And you wanted to find out, if you will, who this person was in the car, didn't you?

OFFICER HOLZER: I wanted to inform the driver of his traffic violation.

MR. EDELSTEIN: Well, you didn't on Columbia Pike, did you?

OFFICER HOLZER: No.

MR. EDELSTEIN: You didn't on Monroe, did you?

OFFICER HOLZER: No.

MR. EDELSTEIN: And you stated your intent was to what, sir?

OFFICER HOLZER: My intent?

MR. EDELSTEIN: Yes.

OFFICER HOLZER: Was to stop the vehicle on a traffic stop.

MR. EDELSTEIN: Did you in fact issue a summons?

OFFICER HOLZER: Yes, I did.

MR. EDELSTEIN: You did? Did you write it there at the scene?

OFFICER HOLZER: No, I wrote it up at the booking area about an hour later.

MR. EDELSTEIN: Did you tell Mr. Alexander that you were there to issue him a summons for a burned-out taillight?

OFFICER HOLZER: I didn't have time to tell him exactly.

MR. EDELSTEIN: So the answer is no, you didn't tell him.

OFFICER HOLZER: No.

MR. EDELSTEIN: Mr. Alexander got out of the car and told you, "This is my house, can I help you."

OFFICER HOLZER: Yes, he said that.

MR. EDELSTEIN: Did you at that time have your radio with you?

OFFICER HOLZER: Yes.

MR. EDELSTEIN: Did you ever run the license number of the car?

OFFICER HOLZER: I didn't have time.

MR. EDELSTEIN: You followed the car for three blocks, didn't you?

OFFICER HOLZER: Yes, well it was a short period of time.

MR. EDELSTEIN: You were able to call backup, weren't you?

OFFICER HOLZER: Yes.

MR. EDELSTEIN: Well, when you called for backup, did you say, "Please check the license number?"

OFFICER HOLZER: No.

MR. EDELSTEIN: Now, did you take steps to confirm whether Mr. Alexander really lived there.

OFFICER HOLZER: Yes, I did.

MR. EDELSTEIN: What was that?

OFFICER HOLZER: I asked him to step back to his car. I approached him with dialogue about where he lived, his driver's license and why I stopped him.

MR. EDELSTEIN: Oh, you say you asked him for his driver's license?

OFFICER HOLZER: I asked him to step back to his car, that's how I would have gotten that information.

MR. EDELSTEIN: My question, sir, is did you say verbally, "Give me your driver's license?"

OFFICER HOLZER: No, I did not.

MR. EDELSTEIN: Now, you're the one that summoned Mr. Alexander to the rear of the car?

OFFICER HOLZER: Yes.

MR. EDELSTEIN: And he complied, didn't he?

OFFICER HOLZER: Yes.

MR. EDELSTEIN: Now did Mr. Alexander raise his hands or do anything to threaten you?

OFFICER HOLZER: He raised his hands in the way he was yelling at me. He was hostile.

MR. EDELSTEIN: When Mr. Alexander was walking back to you, you say he raised his hands. All he did, according to you, was just use his hands to sort of speak, right?

OFFICER HOLZER: Yeah. I wasn't concerned about his hands at that point. It was when he brought them down to his waist.

MR. EDELSTEIN: As he walked toward you, his hands were up and open like mine, right?

OFFICER HOLZER: I believe, yes.

MR. EDELSTEIN: You had your flashlight on him, didn't you?

OFFICER HOLZER: Yes, I did.

MR. EDELSTEIN: So he wasn't holding anything, right?

OFFICER HOLZER: I don't know, no, but I was concerned.

MR. EDELSTEIN: Did you draw your weapon at that time?

OFFICER HOLZER: No.

MR. EDELSTEIN: Did you take any offensive action?

OFFICER HOLZER: No.

MR. EDELSTEIN: But you were concerned for your safety, right?

OFFICER HOLZER: Yes.

MR. EDELSTEIN: Did you say anything to him then?

OFFICER HOLZER: I don't recall if I said anything to him. I think I may have said, "I'm going to pat you down." I always say that before I pat somebody down.

MR. EDELSTEIN: Well, I beg your pardon, just tell us what you said then. We don't want to know what you always do.

OFFICER HOLZER: I don't recall exactly what I said.

MR. EDELSTEIN: In fact, as far as you know, you didn't tell him you were going to pat him down, did you?

OFFICER HOLZER: I don't recall if I did, so I'm going to say, no, I didn't.

MR. EDELSTEIN: Right. How did you pat him down?

OFFICER HOLZER: I reached out my right hand to pat down the area between his fists and the area around his fists.

MR. EDELSTEIN: Did you touch him?

OFFICER HOLZER: No.

MR. EDELSTEIN: How close was he to you?

OFFICER HOLZER: Approximately a foot or a foot and a half.

(Lights bright on Suzanne in hotel room.)

MR. EDELSTEIN: That's pretty much face to face, isn't it?

OFFICER HOLZER: Yes, it is.

MR. EDELSTEIN: And then you say you reached for Mr. Alexander to pat him down, but you didn't tell him so, right?

OFFICER HOLZER: I believe I did, but I don't recall whether I did or not. I believe I did.

MR. EDELSTEIN: You mean you're not sure whether you reached for him?

(Suzanne sees Teddy on the hood of the car, standing in Yorick's grave.)

OFFICER HOLZER: No, I'm not sure exactly what I said to him.

MR. EDELSTEIN: The fact of the matter is you hit him right in the face, didn't you?

OFFICER HOLZER: I hit him after he struck me. I don't recall if I hit him in the face, so to answer your question, I don't recall where I hit him.

(Standing in Yorick's grave, Teddy cries out, "Mom, help me." Fade.)

MR. EDELSTEIN: What hand did you use?

OFFICER HOLZER: I used my right hand.

MR. EDELSTEIN: Didn't you hit him with the flashlight too?

OFFICER HOLZER: No.

MR. EDELSTEIN: You hit him with your right-hand fist?

OFFICER HOLZER: Yes.

MR. EDELSTEIN: You claim he struck you?

OFFICER HOLZER: Yes.

(Trial fades.)

===

*(Suzanne hears her father's friends singing "Let Me Call You
Sweetheart" very softly.*
   Suzanne, sitting in hotel.)

SUZANNE: I dream of a summer evening in Cleveland in the
1940s.

My father and his friends held the meeting of the NAACP
on an old campsite I loved as a child, a place called Aurora,
Ohio.

I walked down a path lined with whitewashed stones.
But seeing into the wooden cabin where my father and his
friends sat was difficult. The Canadian Soldier moths covered the screened door of the cabin. It was Cabin 17.

(Suzanne fades.)

===

(Trial progresses.)

MR. EDELSTEIN: With what hand?

OFFICER HOLZER: The right.

MR. EDELSTEIN: Was it open or closed?

OFFICER HOLZER: I don't recall. It was a quick strike, so I didn't
see whether it was a slap or a fist.

MR. EDELSTEIN: And where did he hit you?

OFFICER HOLZER: The upper left arm, about where my patch is located on my uniform.

MR. EDELSTEIN: Did you feel the blow?

OFFICER HOLZER: Yes.

MR. EDELSTEIN: You did? Did it cause you injury to your body?

OFFICER HOLZER: No.

MR. EDELSTEIN: Did it knock you back?

OFFICER HOLZER: I don't recall, it happened so quick. It may have knocked me back. It was a quick strike.

MR. EDELSTEIN: Have you been assaulted by citizens many times?

OFFICER HOLZER: Sir? No.

MR. EDELSTEIN: So you're telling the court that Mr. Alexander might have struck you with enough force to knock you back and you don't recall?

OFFICER HOLZER: Yes.

MR. EDELSTEIN: So you say he struck you? You didn't tell people that night that he touched you?

OFFICER HOLZER: I may have said that.

MR. EDELSTEIN: Didn't you tell Mr. Alexander's father at the police station that, "He touched me and I don't like being touched"? Didn't you say that?

OFFICER HOLZER: I may have. By saying that, he touched me by striking me. Striking somebody is touching, isn't it?

MR. EDELSTEIN: I don't want to argue with you, sir, but you and I can agree that a touch is different than a strike, isn't it?

OFFICER HOLZER: Touching is when you make body contact with somebody. You can do it by lightly touching or you can do it by hitting with your fist.

(In hotel room, Suzanne walks down stone path toward Cabin 17. Her father's friends' singing is louder. She hears her father whistling.)

MR. EDELSTEIN: So you recall being confronted by Mr. Alexander at the scene after he had found his son placed under arrest?

OFFICER HOLZER: Yes.

MR. EDELSTEIN: And he asked you several times what he did to be arrested?

OFFICER HOLZER: Yes, I recall him asking me several questions.

MR. EDELSTEIN: And you didn't tell him at that time that he had assaulted you, did you?

OFFICER HOLZER: I told him he was under arrest.

MR. EDELSTEIN: No, sir, please hear my question. You didn't tell him —

OFFICER HOLZER: I didn't feel I had to tell him, that he needed to know, so I did not tell him.

(Suzanne stands very still in front of Cabin 17 and listens to her father whistling "Let Me Call You Sweetheart.")

MR. EDELSTEIN: All right. Just so the court understands, you didn't tell Mr. Alexander right at the scene that his son had assaulted you, did you?

OFFICER HOLZER: No.

MR. EDELSTEIN: Now back to the point of contact, if you will, according to you, you were touched once, is that right?

OFFICER HOLZER: I was struck once.

MR. EDELSTEIN: And no blood, no injury, correct?

(Trial fades.)

═══

(Suzanne in hotel room.)

SUZANNE: I'll come back in August when the Canadian Soldiers die. I want to see my father and his friends. I hope when I return to Cabin 17 in August I will hear my father's friends discuss (as they always did) how to make Cleveland a better place for Negroes, how to raise money for the Quincy Library and for the cornerstone ceremony for the Central Y and, as they always did, talk about justice for their children, and Bob Feller.

(She remains standing, staring into Cabin 17. Yorick's grave beyond . . .)

═══

(Trial resumes.)

OFFICER HOLZER: That's correct.
MR. EDELSTEIN: How hard did you hit him?
OFFICER HOLZER: I don't recall.

(Suzanne hears her father say "Justice.")

MR. EDELSTEIN: As hard as you could, didn't you?
OFFICER HOLZER: I don't know. It was a defense mode.
MR. EDELSTEIN: What do you mean a defense mode?
OFFICER HOLZER: I mean, someone struck me and my reaction was to strike him to get away from him assaulting me.
MR. EDELSTEIN: Now, you're a trained police officer, aren't you?
OFFICER HOLZER: Yes.
MR. EDELSTEIN: And aren't you trained to use the least possible force to bring a situation into order?
OFFICER HOLZER: Yes, to conduct an arrest.
MR. EDELSTEIN: That's right. And you could have pulled your weapon and stopped the whole situation, right?
OFFICER HOLZER: That wouldn't have been reasonable. . . . I felt it wouldn't have been reasonable at the time.

MR. EDELSTEIN: But you claim you were struck? In danger.

OFFICER HOLZER: Yes.

MR. EDELSTEIN: Okay. But you didn't pull your weapon?

OFFICER HOLZER: No.

MR. EDELSTEIN: Didn't shoot your mace?

OFFICER HOLZER: No.

=====

(In hotel room, Suzanne sees March walking.)

MARCH: The Bay Bridge is fallen. We live near the epicenter.

(March exits.)

=====

MR. EDELSTEIN: Didn't use that flashlight?

OFFICER HOLZER: No.

MR. EDELSTEIN: You hit him again after the first time, didn't you?

OFFICER HOLZER: Yes. I struck him and then grabbed him and threw him to the ground, directed him to the ground.

MR. EDELSTEIN: Where did you strike him this time?

OFFICER HOLZER: Well, I grabbed him and held onto him. It wasn't a strike. And I placed him on the ground.

MR. EDELSTEIN: Well, you didn't place him to the ground, you kicked him and knocked him to the ground, didn't you?

OFFICER HOLZER: I did not.

MR. EDELSTEIN: Didn't you kick him about the chest and body?

OFFICER HOLZER: Not at that point.

MR. EDELSTEIN: When did you do that?

OFFICER HOLZER: When he started to resist, when I had one handcuff on him.

(In hotel room, Suzanne stares after March, then again stares back at Cabin 17.)

MR. EDELSTEIN: What did he do to resist?

OFFICER HOLZER: Tried to get away from me, pushed away.

MR. EDELSTEIN: He tried to escape?

OFFICER HOLZER: Yes, he was resisting being placed in custody. He flung his arms around and pushed away.

MR. EDELSTEIN: Did he hit you again?

OFFICER HOLZER: No.

MR. EDELSTEIN: And you were punching and kicking him and dragging him across the drive?

OFFICER HOLZER: I was trying to subdue him.

MR. EDELSTEIN: Kicking and punching him?

OFFICER HOLZER: I don't recall. It's possible. Anything's possible.

MR. EDELSTEIN: You didn't like his attitude?

OFFICER HOLZER: No. I mean, I wish he would have been cooperative.

MR. EDELSTEIN: Now, during the time you had him on the ground, you said you kicked him?

OFFICER HOLZER: Yes.

MR. EDELSTEIN: Where did you kick him?

OFFICER HOLZER: In the upper body.

MR. EDELSTEIN: And how many times did you kick him?

OFFICER HOLZER: I would say about three times.

MR. EDELSTEIN: All right, sir. Don't you recall that when you hit him first that he was stunned and dropped to the ground of his own accord?

OFFICER HOLZER: No.

MR. EDELSTEIN: Don't you recall that he not only didn't but couldn't offer any resistance?

OFFICER HOLZER: He offered plenty of resistance.

MR. EDELSTEIN: Did you ever hit the ground?

OFFICER HOLZER: No.

MR. EDELSTEIN: You were on top and he was on the bottom.

OFFICER HOLZER: Correct.

MR. EDELSTEIN: Now were you treated for any injuries after the assault?

OFFICER HOLZER: No.

MR. EDELSTEIN: Was there any mark on your uniform from this blow?

OFFICER HOLZER: No, I didn't see any marks.

MR. EDELSTEIN: And did you keep it secure for evidence purposes?

OFFICER HOLZER: I saw no need.

MR. EDELSTEIN: And just so the court can understand, this touching or blow, you don't even know whether the hand was open or closed, do you?

OFFICER HOLZER: It happened so fast, I couldn't see.

MR. EDELSTEIN: Faster than Muhammad Ali, right, it was so quick?

OFFICER HOLZER: I don't know if it was that fast.

MR. EDELSTEIN: Right. Are you sure it happened at all, Officer?

OFFICER HOLZER: I'm positive it happened. We wouldn't be here if it didn't.

MR. EDELSTEIN: But you didn't tell Mr. Alexander on the scene that it happened.

OFFICER HOLZER: I didn't have to.

MR. EDELSTEIN: You didn't want to.

OFFICER HOLZER: I didn't have to. He was belligerent so I was not going to tell him anything. He was half naked, too.

MR. EDELSTEIN: The point is you didn't tell him.

=====

(In hotel. March walks on. He calls again.)

MARCH: We live near the epicenter.

(He vanishes. Suzanne is again staring at Yorick's grave.)

=====

OFFICER HOLZER: No, I didn't. I wouldn't tell anybody like that, no.

MR. EDELSTEIN: Even after you locked up his own son in his front yard?

OFFICER HOLZER: That's correct. I didn't know it was his front yard.

MR. EDELSTEIN: Okay, but you didn't even bother to find out, did you?

OFFICER HOLZER: It had nothing to do with anything.

MR. EDELSTEIN: You didn't see Mr. Alexander come out of a house wearing a night shirt?

OFFICER HOLZER: Yes.

MR. EDELSTEIN: That's all the questions I have. Thank you.

JUDGE: There are no further questions?

MS. WAGNER: No, ma'am. Your Honor, that would be the commonwealth's evidence in its case.

MR. EDELSTEIN: May I be heard?

JUDGE: You may.

(Trial fades.)

=====

(Lights on Teddy. He remembers:)

OFFICER HOLZER *(Yelling)*: Get back in the car.

(Teddy opens the door.)

OFFICER HOLZER *(He has moved closer to Teddy and is standing at the back of the car)*: Come back here.

(Teddy consciously places his arms at his side away from his body and slowly walks toward Officer Holzer. He is petrified and stares at the gun in the Officer's holster. Officer Holzer stands at the back of the car shining his flashlight at Teddy. He grabs Teddy's right hand and tries to yank him to the ground. Teddy pulls his arm away.)

TEDDY: Don't touch me.

(Teddy is hit with a heavy blow to the left side of his face with the flashlight. His knees buckle and he crumples to the ground. Officer Holzer grabs Teddy's right arm and begins to drag him across the driveway, repeatedly kicking and punching Teddy in his head, upper body and back.

  David Jr. comes running out of the house and sees his brother being beaten.)

VOICE OF DAVID JR.: Police, a police officer is beating up my brother, please send help. 5943 Riverdale Road.
  (Yells) Dad, the police are beating up Teddy.

(Spotlight shines on Teddy. After dragging Teddy diagonally across the cement drive Officer Holzer slams Teddy's face down to the ground. Teddy lands on the dirt and wet leaves, his head just inches away from smashing into a cluster of large rocks. Officer Holzer pulls Teddy's right arm upward and kicks him several more times in his chest and then places the handcuffs on him. Another officer appears and helps Officer Holzer pull Teddy up.

  David Alexander follows David Jr. out of the house and stands in the front yard. The officers place Teddy spread-eagle, his upper body placed flat on the car, his face turned sideways, his legs spread wide open, on top of the front of a police car. Two more officers surround Teddy, pinning him down on the hood of the car. Teddy is dazed and can barely breathe.

David Jr. in background quietly films this with camcorder.)

TEDDY: I can't breathe, could you please let me up.

(Officer Holzer places more pressure on Teddy's back and ignores his plea for help.)

TEDDY: I can't breathe. I am an American citizen, please let me up. I can't breathe, please. . . .

(Teddy tries to raise his chest off the hood of the car several inches so he can breathe, as he does one of the officers punches him very hard in the kidney area. Teddy yells out in pain as they push him back onto the hood.)

DAVID ALEXANDER: Stop hurting him.
TEDDY: Dad, dad!
DAVID ALEXANDER: What is going on?

(David Alexander and David Jr. move toward the scene. A Police Woman pulls out her revolver, pointing it at them.)

POLICE WOMAN: Stay right where you are.
DAVID ALEXANDER: What is going on? What are you doing to my son?
OFFICER HOLZER: He is being arrested.
DAVID ALEXANDER: For what?

(Officer Holzer walks away.)

DAVID ALEXANDER: For what? What's the charge?

(Officer Holzer moves Teddy to the paddy wagon.)

TEDDY: Why am I being arrested? What is the charge?

DAVID ALEXANDER: You can't arrest him without a charge....
What's the charge?...Will someone answer me? What's the
charge?

TEDDY: What have I done?

DAVID ALEXANDER: Who's in charge here? What's your name? I
am talking to you.

(Officer Holzer pays very little attention to David Alexander.)

DAVID ALEXANDER: What's your name? What's your name and
what's the charge?

OFFICER HOLZER: You will be told at the station.

DAVID ALEXANDER: At the station? I want to know now, don't you
have to tell somebody why you are arresting him?

OFFICER HOLZER: I told him.

TEDDY: You never told me. Why am I being arrested?

DAVID ALEXANDER: Why is he being arrested?

OFFICER HOLZER: If there is a problem, you can talk to the night
supervisor.

(Teddy is placed into the paddy wagon.)

DAVID ALEXANDER: I will. David Jr., do you have a pen and
paper? . . . What's your name and number?

OFFICER HOLZER: It's right here on my uniform, can't you see it?

DAVID ALEXANDER: It's dark and you keep moving around. What
is it? *(He tries to read the officer's badge)* . . . Holzer . . .
892462 . . . you have made a very big mistake, my friend.
You have tangled with the wrong family. You are going to be
very sorry.

(Fade.)

(Trial resumes.)

MR. EDELSTEIN: Thank you. Your Honor, at this time, on behalf
of the defendant, Teddy Alexander, I would move to strike
the charge which has been brought against him. As I said in
the opening statement, in the long run this case is really
about a police assault upon Mr. Alexander, and the officer
conceded that. But I want to focus on what the alleged
assault here is. As I read the charge, it's assault and battery.

The officer now tells us that he doesn't even remember
telling him he was going to pat him down. All he has to offer
the court is a claim that he was assaulted by being touched
on his shoulder by what we have established on cross-
examination is an open hand. Now I believe, Your Honor
must find first of all as a matter of law that that's not suffi-
cient given the circumstances. We have a law enforcement
officer fully prepared to protect himself, fully able to do so,
and under the circumstances, has no corroborative evidence whatsoever, no injury, no treatment, no preserved
evidence, no pictures and nothing of the sort to show this
court that an assault in fact occurred.

After that, of course, we have what amounts to a beating,
and nobody in this courtroom can doubt that that happened.
But my client is charged with committing an assault upon
an officer.

Where's the battery? There's no other hitting. There's no
other striking. The state is not charging any other offensive
behavior by Mr. Alexander. And we suggest that the case
has to be dismissed at this point.

And I would add, Your Honor, you're the finder of fact
here, and I would say that the credibility of this officer on
that point is not worthy of belief. I submit first of all it didn't

happen. It's not credible that it happened. But, even if the testimony is credited by the court, as a matter of law, it can't survive this motion.

MS. WAGNER: Well, Your Honor, I'm sure counsel knows that assault and battery is an unlawful touching, however slight, done in an angry, rude or vengeful manner.

Now putting that aside for a minute, the testimony is unrebutted that the officer was struck by this defendant after a course of conduct that the officer testified to as belligerent, uncooperative, not responding to his request that he get back into the car, that he started to walk toward the officer, and at that point the officer went to pat him down.

And it was at that point that the assaultive behavior began by this defendant, and the officer responded as only this officer could. The officer had a right to arrest that man for the assault. He was assaulted on that morning and that's why he arrested him. And I ask that the court not grant the motion to strike and proceed with the evidence in this case.

JUDGE: The court hesitates to comment on any of the rationale for its decision, but would say I'm going to grant the motion to strike only because I hold police officers to a higher standard and expect an assault to constitute more than what I have heard. Case dismissed. *(Scene fades)*

(Lights on Suzanne in hotel. Yorick's grave vanishes. Lights fade on Suzanne.

Bright light on Teddy, sitting alone in courtroom. He remembers his family at the table in Edelstein's office watching film of his beating. The film is very dark and filled with the sounds of his screams.)

END OF PLAY

ADAM P. KENNEDY is a writer and producer. He was born in Rome, Italy, and grew up in New York City. He attended Riverdale Country School and Antioch College, where he majored in International Relations and Journalism. Mr. Kennedy has lived and traveled in Europe, Africa, the Middle East and the South Pacific. His television production company, R.A.V.E., has produced shows for teens that have aired nationally on PBS and network television, including "Africa/USA: The Connection," in 1991; "The World Connection," a three-part series, in 1992–93; and "Phat Traks," a weekly hip-hop music program, in 1994. R.A.V.E's most recent TV projects include an espionage drama and a children's program. Mr. Kennedy has just completed his first novel, *The Congo Affair*, a 1960s political thriller, and *The Curia*, a screenplay.

ADRIENNE KENNEDY was born in Pittsburgh and now makes her home in New York City. Her best known plays are *Funnyhouse of a Negro*, *A Movie Star Has to Star in Black and White* and *The Owl Answers*. She received a 1996 Obie Award for *June and Jean in Concert* and, with her son, Adam Kennedy, received the 1996 Obie Award for Best Play for *Sleep Deprivation Chamber*, which premiered at New York's Public Theater and was produced by Signature Theatre Company, which devoted an entire year-long season to Ms. Kennedy's work. Her plays are taught in colleges throughout this country, Europe, India and Africa, and she has been a visiting lecturer at New York University, University of California at Berkeley and Harvard. She has received numerous awards including a Guggenheim award, the Lila Wallace Readers Digest Award and the American Academy of Arts and Letters Award for Literature. Her published work includes *In One Act*, *Alexander Plays* and *Deadly Triplets* all published by University of Minnesota Press, and *People Who Led to My Plays*, a memoir, published by Theatre Communications Group. A study of her work, *Intersecting Boundaries: Theatre of Adrienne Kennedy* has also been published by University of Minnesota Press.